Dear Future, I'm Ready

Copyright © 2024 **Dreamanifeel** Publishing

All Rights Reserved.

LOVE

True Love

I Always Will love you

LOVE YOU

Me You

I LOVE my Family

FAMILY

family =first=

Family Work

HOBBY

START

NEW JOB

GiRL BOSS

WORK TiME

BUSINESS

Work **HARD** Dream **BIG**

designed by 🜲 freepik

CAREER

Married
LIFE

Just
Married

Mr. & Mrs.

WEEDING

BRIDE

Baby ♥
IN PROGRESS

PREGNANT

HAVE A BABY

All Bodies
-are-
Beautiful

Life is Better with cats

I LOVE my DOGS

My Body My Rules

NEVER give up

FITNESS

you can Do this.

your BODY is a Reflection of your Lifestyle

Perfect BODY LOADING WORKOUT

Ready FOR NEW *ADVENTURES*

TRAVEL THE WORLD

I ♥ TRAVEL

VACATION

TRAVEL

HOME

NEW HOME

HOME IS WHERE THE LOVE IS

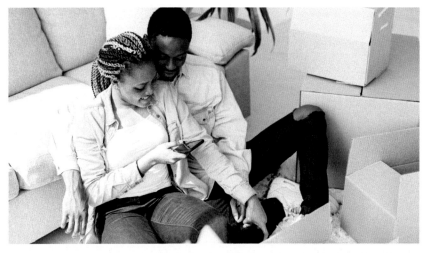

SAVE MONEY

DEBT FREE

DEBT   PROFIT

YOUR NAME
Street, Town
Tel : (001) 100-00000

0001

DATE _____

PAY TO THE
ORDER OF _____ $ [   ]

_____ DOLLARS 🔒

FOR _____   _____

⑆123456789O⑈ ⑆123456789O ⑆OOO1

MONEY FLOWS

FINANCIAL
Freedom
AWAITS

ABUNDANC

YOUR NAME
Street Town
Tel : (001) 444-00000

0001

DATE _____

PAY TO THE
ORDER OF _____ $ [   ]

_____ DOLLARS Security features included Details on back 🔒

BANK NAME
Street, Town
Tel : (001) 444-00000

FOR _____   _____

⑆ O12345678 ⑆ OOO123456789 ⑆ OOO1

LIFE IS
BETTER
with
FRIENDS

Better together

FRIENDS
FORE♥ER

FRIENDSHIP

MY Bookish ERA

CRAZY BOOK lady

READ MORE BOOKS

BOOKS because REALITY is BORING

SELF CARE

SELF CARE ISN'T SELFISH

BEAUTY

take care of yourself

GRADUATION

CLASS OF 2025

EDUCATION KNOWS NO LIMITS

GLAD TO BE A GRAD
2024

study

Congratulations

LEARNING

EAT FOR HEALTH

HEALTHY FOOD

KETO DIET

5%
25%
70%

■ - CARBS ■ - PROTEIN ■ - FATS

LOSE WEIGHT

Get Fit

HEALTH

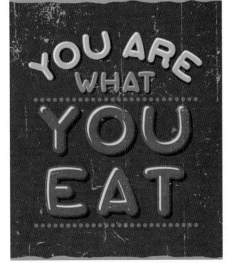

YOU ARE WHAT YOU EAT

MEDITATION

SPIRITUALITY

Pray MORE Worry Less

GOD

Faith

Thankful GRATEFUL BLESSED

PRAY THEN LET IT GO

2025

GOALS

POSSIBLE

SUCCESS

DISCIPLINE
~not desire~
DETERMINES
~destiny~

dream big work hard

2025

STOP DREAMING START Doing

Time TO Reach YOUR GOALS

LIFE BEGINS at the end OF YOUR CONFORT zone.

HEALTHY HABITS

DRINK MORE WATER

SLEEP WELLNESS

MEANS NO!

Mental **HEALTH**

STOP Smoking Quit

NO JUNK FOOD AREA

Yoga Heals THE Soul

Just Breathe

REACH YOUR BALANCE

WORRY LESS Yoga MORE

YOGA

YOGA is your LIFE

more **Self Love**

YOU ARE -SO- LOVED

Loose your way and find your Soul

SELF LOVE

My Goals for 2025

Health & Wellness Goals

- ♡ _____
- ♡ _____
- ♡ _____
- ♡ _____
- ♡ _____

Personal Development Goals

- ♡ _____
- ♡ _____
- ♡ _____
- ♡ _____
- ♡ _____

Spiritual Goals

- ♡ _____
- ♡ _____
- ♡ _____
- ♡ _____
- ♡ _____

Relationship & Social Goals

- ♡ _____
- ♡ _____
- ♡ _____
- ♡ _____
- ♡ _____

Career & Professional Goals

- ♡ _____
- ♡ _____
- ♡ _____
- ♡ _____
- ♡ _____

Financial Goals

- ♡ _____
- ♡ _____
- ♡ _____
- ♡ _____
- ♡ _____

THIS YEAR I WILL :

Quit

Start

Travel

Honor

Learn

Be

Commit

Act

Eat

Accept

Give

Have

Forgive

Dream	Hope	Grateful	Joy
Save	Be Aware	Sexy	Optimism
Progress	Beautiful	Focus	Build
Be Kind	Successful	Peace	Passion
Balance	Kids	The Best	Stress Less
Power	I'm Ready	Rich	Change
Discipline	Study	Fun	Explore
Calm	Mindset	Wealth	School
Provide	Controlled	Strong	Lifestyle
Pleasure	Take Risks	Boss	Consistent
Look Better	Decisive	Style	Committed

Do what you love

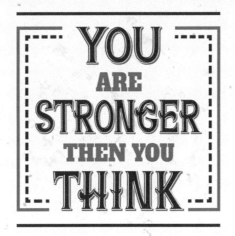

YOU ARE STRONGER THEN YOU THINK

NEVER give up YOUR DREAMS

BE The best version OF YOU

YOU'RE BEAUTIFUL capable worthy

Do it with passion or NOT at ALL!

Belive in yourself

Always dream Big

you ARE WORTHY

SHINE LIKE A STAR

I AM ENOUGH

Don't Be AFRAID To Be GREAT

ENJOY
WHEN YOU CAN
&
ENDURE
WHEN YOU MUST

Be the Change that you want to see in the world

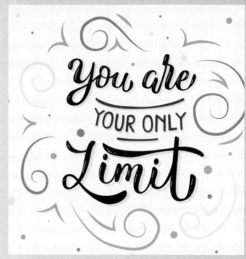

You are
YOUR ONLY
Limit

MISTAKES
are proof
THAT YOU ARE
Trying

Remember
WHY
You Started

FIND A
Balance

You are an
AWESOME
HUMAN
BEING

Never
LOSE
Hope

Let your
DREAMS
be your
Wings

IF YOU
BELIEVE
in it
THEN
FIGHT
for it

DON'T
FORCE
yourself
to
FIT IN
where YOU
DON'T belong

BE PROUD
OF
YOURSELF

Made in United States
Orlando, FL
30 December 2024

56710362R00033